CURRICULUM PLANNING AND DEVELOPMENT

Dr. Paresh B. Acharya

M.Sc. (Maths), M.Ed., M.Phil., Ph.D., NET.

Assistant professor
Shri I. J. Patel M. Ed. Course
Mogri, Anand, India

CANADIAN
Academic Publishing

2014

Price : $27.86

First Edition : 2014

ISBN : 978-1-926488-21-9

ISBN Allotment Agency : Library and Archives Canada (Govt. of Canada)

Published & Printed by
Canadian Academic Publishing
81, Woodlot Crescent,
Etobicoke,
Toronto, Ontario, Canada.
Postal Code- M9W 6T3
Phone- +1 (647) 633 9712
http://www.canadapublish.com

PREFACE

Curriculum document is a comprehensive plan of any educational program. It is also one of the means for bringing about qualitative improvement in any program. A crucial part of a curriculum reform initiative involves the practice of Improving Learning, Teaching, and Assessment for All Students. . Curriculum work is an essential function of leadership in schools because it is through the curriculum development process that we identify purpose, define an activity, and rationalize decision making in schools. Our goal in writing Developmentally Appropriate Curriculum in Action is to provide you with the professional knowledge and skills you will need to be an effective secondary school teacher. The material in this text has been thoroughly principles, making use of the latest theories and findings about how students and about how great teachers teach. This text presents models, ideas, examples, and theories to prod critical reflections leading to proxies that acknowledge local/global contexts, cultures, and conceptual frameworks. Teachers of Education can use this book to develop the curriculum in their stream. University faculty can use this book to facilitate powwow regarding theoretical and operational curriculum issues, specifically when contemplating the role of curriculum development in teacher education. This book contains six chapters in order. Chapters1 address theoretical foundations and a set of concepts for analyzing the field for the development of curricula. Chapter 2, a sense of aims, objectives and principles is very important for anyone working in the curriculum. Without an understanding of this, many contemporary curriculum practices would seem odd or even illogical. Chapter three related with the best approach to curriculum design is to combine the best of both approaches according to student need, teacher experience and organizational structure and resources. Resources include people, instructional materials, supplies and equipment. Chapter four provides curriculum development. Chapter five, this book provides teaching-learning models that can be used in the development and implementation of a curriculum. Teacher education and school education have a symbiotic relationship.

Developments in both these sectors mutually reinforce the concerns necessary for the qualitative improvement of the entire spectrum of education. So fulfill the purpose of this included chapter six reviews of NCF.

I hope the book will help provide an understanding of some deep and fundamental insights from curriculum theory.

- Dr. Paresh B. Acharya

CONTENTS

CHAPTER - 1
MEANING OF CURRICULUM

Curriculum and Syllabus: The two terms curriculum and syllabus have several meanings and different definitions. In addition, there is confusion between these two terms. Curriculum and Syllabus have been defined according to educators' philosophical tendencies, .psychological and linguistic assumptions. J. C.Aggarawall (1996:307-16)Principles, Methods & Techniques of teaching "declared that the meaning of curriculum is totality of all the learning to which students are exposed during their study in school. He has listed 79 definitions in his book (Curriculum Reforms in India 1990). Some of the most important definitions are as follows Alberty, A. and Alberty, E. (1959) regard curriculum as "the sum total of students' activities which the school sponsors for the purpose of achieving its Objectives. Curriculum as defined in A Dictionary of Education by Rowntree Derek (1981) Curriculum can refer to the total structure of ideas and activities developed by an educational institution to meet the learning needs of students and to achieve desired educational aims." Dictionary of Education (1973) edited by Carter V. Good

1

gives the meaning of curriculum as: "Curriculum is a body of prescribed experiences under school supervision, designed to provide an individual with the possible training and experience to fit him for all society of which he is a part or to qualify him for a trade or profession." A Dictionary of Education (1982) by P. J. Hills defines the curriculum "a simple way of considering the curriculum is to see in terms of four facets: content, methods, purposes, evaluation".

Definitions of curriculum Standard dictionaries define curriculum as a course of study offered by an academic institution. According to Ronald Doll, curriculum is the formal and informal content and process by which learners gain knowledge and understanding, develop skills, and alter attitudes, appreciations, and values under the auspices of an academic institution. In other words, curriculum can be defined as the total experience. From this view point, Curriculum is not only the content selected and delivered, but also the planned and unplanned activities in which individuals' participate as students. In educational literature, in short, the word curriculum has been defined in the following ways: "Curriculum is such "permanent" subjects as grammar, reading, logic, rhetoric, mathematics and the greatest books of the Western world that embody essential knowledge". "Curriculum is those subjects that are most useful for living in contemporary society". "Curriculum is all planned learning for which the institution is responsible". "Curriculum is all the experiences learners have under the guidance of the institution". "Curriculum is the totality of learning experiences provided to students so that they can attain general skills and knowledge at a variety of learning sites". "Curriculum is a structured series of intended learning outcomes". The other terms that are commonly used as synonymous to curriculum are syllabus and course. But curriculum can refer to any level of an educational experience, from that of a particular area within a course, to the course itself, to a broader program of study that comprises a number of different courses around a particular content area. Curriculum is often used to refer to a focus of study, consisting of various courses all designed to reach a particular proficiency or qualification; Syllabus refers to the content or subject matter, instructional strategies and evaluation means of an individual course. The collective syllabus of a program of study represents a map of the curriculum for that program. A curriculum is developed through planning for a larger program of study and then building syllabi for courses to manifest the curriculum design and plan. However, even developing a syllabus for a specific course can be thought of as a form of curriculum development.

Different Meaning of Curriculum:

1. Liberal Meaning: The term curriculum is of Latin origin and it implies an athletic ground, thus indicating that curriculum is the ground 'through which the educand has to pass in order to reach a definite goal. In the past, the term was taken to mean a collection of knowledge and skill. It did not then imply to educand's needs, but instead the knowledge and skill of the specialists working in different spheres.

2. Modern interpretation: Bent and Kronenbuag suggest, that the curriculum is the organized form of subject matter, specially prepared experiences and activities which provide the student with the knowledge and the skill he will require in facing the various situations of real life. Obviously, the term 'curriculum' cannot be restricted to a list of books, because it must include other activities which provide the student with the knowledge and the skill he will require in facing the various situations of life. Meet the requirements of children. Hence, now curriculum includes those the environment of the schools and numerous other elements not taught by books. In the words of Bent and Kronenburg, "Curriculum, in its broadest sense, includes the complete school environment, involving all the courses, activities, reading and associations furnished to the pupils in the school."

3. Curriculum as experience: In the words of Munroe, "Curriculum embodies all the experience which is utilized by the school to attain the aims of education." Thus, the various subjects included for study in a curriculum are not intended merely for study or rote learning but to convey experiences of various kinds. The concept has been defined in more or less the same terms in the report of the Secondary Education Commission in these words, "Curriculum does not mean only the academic subject traditionally taught it the school, but in includes the totality of experiences that a pupil receives through the manifold activities that go oh in the school in the classroom, library, laboratory, workshop, playgrounds and in the numerous informal contacts between teachers and pupils." Another definition of curriculum as experience is provided by Crow and Crow, "The curriculum includes all the learner's experiences in or outside school that are included in a programme which has been devised to help him develop mentally, physically,, emotionally, socially, spiritually and morally." It is obvious, then that the aim of curriculum is to provide' experience to the educand so that he may achieve complete development. By calling the curriculum an. experience, the fact is made explicit that it includes not merely books, but all those activities and relationship which are indulged in by the educand, both inside and outside the school. Hence, the syllabi specified by the authority should not be taken to mean curriculum.

4. Curriculum as a means of tool: It is apparent from the foregoing definitions that curriculum is not an end in itself, but a means to an end because it is created in order to achieve the aims of education. That is why one finds that different educationists have suggested different kinds of curricula to conform to the aims and objectives ascribed to education. Explaining the concept of curriculum as a tool of education, Cunningham writes, "The curriculum is the tool in the hands of the artist (the teacher) to mould his material (the pupil) according to his ideal (objective) in his studio (the school)." Here the educators are compared to an artist and the curriculum as one of the instruments of tools used by him to develop the educand according to, and in conformity with the aims of education. It is evident that the curriculum will change with every change in the aims of education. **5. Curriculum as environment:** The most comprehensive definition of curriculum is given by those who conceive it to include the total environment of the school. In the words of H. L.Caswell, "The curriculum is all that goes on in the lives of the children, their parents and their teachers. The curriculum is made up of everything that surrounds the learner in all 'his working hours." I fact, the curriculum has been described as "the environment in motion." In modern times, the term is interpreted in this more liberal sense because there is no questioning the fact that the child's education is influenced, by not only books but the playgrounds, library, laboratory, reading room, extracurricular, programmes, - the educational environment, and a host of other factors. In the school, both the educator and the educand are part of the curriculum because they are part of the environment, while in the family the child is expected to progress and achieve the goals of

education.

6. Curriculum includes all activities: It is stated in the Twenty ninth year Book of 'the National Society for the Study of Education, U.S.A. that, "The curriculum may be defined as the totality of, subject matter, activities, and experiences which constitute a pupil's school life." Elaborating the same concept further, H.H. Home says. "The curriculum is that which the pupil is taught. It involves more than the acts of learning and, quiet study, it involves occupations, production, achievements, exercise, and activity." Pragmatists, too, have included the entire range of the educand's activities in the curriculum because according to them, the child learns by doing.

In the light of the various definitions of curriculum given above, it is possible to arrive at a definition of the term which includes all the points mentioned in these definitions. Briefly, then, curriculum is the means of achieving the goals of education. It includes all those experiences, activities and environments which the educand receives during his educational career. Such a definition of curriculum comprehends the educand's entire life, a contention borne out by all modem educationists who believe that the child learns not only inside the school, but also outside it, on the playground, at home, in society, in fact, everywhere. That is why there is nowadays so much insistence on the participation of the parents in the child's education and on not restricting the environment of the curriculum to the school environment but taking it means every possible kind of environment encountered by the child. Besides, it includes all those activities which the child does, irrespective of the time and place of these activities. It also includes the entire range of experiences that the child has in the school, at home, in the world at large. Considering from his liberal standpoint, one finds that is preparing the curriculum one has much wider background than would otherwise be possible.

CHAPTER - 2
AIMS, OBJECTIVES AND PRINCIPLES OF CURRICULUM

The Aims and Objectives of Curriculum Clarifying the aims and objectives of curriculum, it has been pointed out in the report of the Secondary Education Commission that, "The starting point for curricular reconstruction must, therefore, be the device to bridge the gulf between the school subjects and to enrich the varied activities that make up the warp and woof of life." Hence, the curricular should be so designed that it strains the educand to face the situations of real life, a curriculum can be said to have the following major objectives:

1. **Synthesis of subjects and life:** The aim of the curriculum is to arrange and provide those subjects for an educand's study which will enable the educand to destroy any gulf between school life and life outside the school. The opinion of the Secondary Education Commission has already been quoted.

2. **Development of democratic values:** In all democratic countries, the curriculum of education must aim to develop the democratic values of equality, liberty and fraternity, so that the educands may develop into fine democratic

citizens. But the development should not only aim at national benefit. The curriculum must also aim to introducing a spirit of internationalism in the educand.

3. Satisfaction of the educand's need: In defining curriculum, many educationists have insisted that it must be designed to satisfy the needs and requirements of the educand. It is seen that one finds a great variety of interests, skills, abilities, attitudes, aptitudes, etc., among educands. A curriculum should be so designed as to satisfy the general and specific requirements of the educands.

4. Realization of values: One aim of education is development of character, and what is required for this is to create in the educand a faith in the various desirable values. Hence, one of the objectives of education is to create in the educand a definite realization of the prevailing system of values.

5. Development of knowledge: In its most common connotation, the term curriculum is taken to mean development of knowledge or acquisition of facts and very frequently, this is the aspect kept in mind while designing a curriculum. But it must be remembered that it is not the only objective, although it is the most fundamental objective of a curriculum.

6. Creation of a useful environment: Another objective of curriculum is to create an environment suitable to the educand. Primarily the environment must assist the educand in achieving the maximum possible development of his facilities, abilities and capabilities. **7. Addition to knowledge**: In the contemporary educational patterns that curriculum is believed to the suitable which can create a harmony between the various branches of knowledge so that the educand's attitude should be comprehensive and complete, not one sided. **8. Harmony between individual and activity**: In a democracy, such social qualities as social skills, cooperation, the desire to be of service, sympathy, etc., are very significant because without them, no society can continue to exist. On the other hand, development of the individual's own character and personality are also very important. Hence, the curriculum must create an environment and provide those books which enable the individual to achieve his own development at the same time as he learns these social qualities.

Principles of curriculum construction: Principles of Curriculum Construction Different educationists have expressed their own views about the fundamental principles of curriculum construction, the difference being created by their different philosophies of education. Briefly, the main principles of curriculum construction are the following:

1. Principle of utility: T.P.Nunn, the educationist, believes that the principles of utility is the most important principle underlying the formation of a curriculum. He writes, "While the plain man generally likes his children to pick up some scraps of useless learning for purely decorative purpose, he requires, on the whole, that they shall be taught what will be useful to them in later life, and he is inclined to give 'useful' a rather strict interpretation." As a general rule, parents are in favor of including all those subjects in the curriculum which are likely to prove useful for their child in his life, and by means of which he can be made a responsible member of society.

2. Training in the proper patterns of conduct: According to Crow and Crow, the main principle underlying the construction of a curriculum is that, through education the educand should be able to adopt the patterns of behaviour proper to different circumstances. Man is a social animal who has to constantly adapt himself to the social environment. Therefore education must aim at developing all these qualities in the educand which will facilitate this adaptation to the social milieu. The child is by nature self-centered, but education must teach him to attend the needs and requirements of others besides himself. One criterion of an educated individual is that he should be able to adapt himself to different situations with which he is confronted. In this context, the term conduct must be understood in its widest sense. Only then can this principle of curriculum construction be properly. "All out activities in social, economic, family and cultural environment constitute behaviour or conduct, and it is the function of education of teach us how he behave in different situation."

3. Synthesis of play and work: Of the various modern techniques of education, some try to educate through work and others through play. But a great majority of educationists agree that the curriculum should aim at achieving a balance between play and work. In other words, the work given to the educand should be performed in such a manner that the child may believe it to be play. There is a difference between work and play. That is why parents want to engage the child in work instead of allowing him to play all the time, but the child is maturely inclined to spend his time in playing. Keeping this in view, T.P. Nunn has written, "The school should be thought of not as a knowledge-monger's shop, but a place where the young are disciplined in certain forms of activity. All subjects should be taught in the 'plays way' care being taken that the 'way' leads continuously from the irresponsible frolic of childhood to the disciplined labours of manhood."

4. Synthesis of all activities of life: In framing a curriculum, attention should be paid to the inclusion, in it, of all the various activities of life, such as contemplation, learning, acquisition of various kinds of skill, etc. In the individual and social sphere of life, every individual has to perform a great variety of activities, and his success in life is determined by the success of all these activities. Hence, the curriculum should not neglect any form of activity related to any aspect of life. A curriculum constructed on this basis will be both comprehensive and closely related to life. In order words, it should include all the activities that the educand is likely to require in later life.

5. Principle, of individual differences: Modern educational psychology has brought to light, and stressed the significance of individual differences that exist between one individual and another. It has been discovered that people differ in respect of their mental processes, interests, aptitudes, attitudes, abilities, skills, etc., and the these difference are innate. All modern education is paidocentric, that is it is centered around the child. Psychologists insist that the curriculum should be so designed as to provide an opportunity for complete and comprehensive development to widely differing individuals. One of the basic qualities of such a curriculums flexibility; for it must be flexible in order to accommodate educands of low, average or high intelligence and ability, and to provide each one a chance to develop all .his abilities to the greatest possible extent.

6. Constant development: Another basis for curriculum construction is the principle of a dynamic curriculum, based on the realization that no curriculum can prove adequate for all times and in all places. For this reason, the curriculum should be flexible and changeable. This is all the more true in the modern context when new discoveries in the various branches of science are taking place every day. Hence, it becomes necessary to reshape the curriculum fairly, frequently in order to incorporate the latest developments.

7. Creative training: Another important principle of curriculum construction is that of creative training. Raymont has correctly stated that a curriculum appropriate for the needs of today and the future must definitely have a positive bias towards creative subjects. And, one of the aims of education is to develop the creative faculty of the educand. All that is finest in human culture is the creation of man's creative abilities. Children differ from each other in respect of this ability. Hence, in framing a curriculum, attention must be paid to the fact that it should encourage each educand to develop his creative ability as far as is possible.

8. Variety: Variety is another important principle of curriculum construction. The innate complexity of man and many facets of his personality make it necessary that the curriculum should be valid, because no one kind of curriculum can develop all the facilities of an individual. Hence, at every level the curriculum must have variety, it will, on the one hand, provide an opportunity for development of the different faculties of the educand, while on the other, it will retain his interest in education.

9. Education for leisure: One of the objectives ascribed to education is training for leisure, because it is believed that education is not merely for employment or work. Hence, it is desirable that the curriculum should also include training in those activities which will make the individual's leisure more pleasurable. A great variety of social, artistic and sporting activities can be included in this kind of training. Besides, educands should be encouraged to foster some or the other hobby so that they can put their leisure to constructive and pleasant use.

10. Related to community life: Curriculum can also be based on the principle that school and community life must be intimately related to each other. One cannot forget that the school is only a miniature form of community. Hence, the school curriculum should include all those activities which are performed by members of larger community outside the boundaries of the school. This will help in evolving social qualities of the individual, in developing the social aspect of his personality and finally, in helping his final adaptation to the social environment into which he must ultimately go.

11. Evolution of democratic values: The construction of a curriculum in a democratic society is conditioned by the need to develop democratic qualities in the individual. The curriculum should be so designed that it develops a democratic feeling and creates a positive faith in democratic values. The programmes devise in the college qualities in the educand so that he may be able to participate usefully and successfully in democratic life. In all the democratic societies of the world, this is the chief consideration in shaping the curricula for primary, secondary and higher education. It is evident from the foregoing account of the various bases of curriculum construction that this should be duly conditioned by careful thinking on all aspects individual and social life variety, play and work, earning of livelihood, leisure, etc.

CHAPTER - 3
SOURCES OF CURRICULUM CONTENT

The determinants or foundations of curriculum are those basic forces that influence the content and organization; they include studies of the nature and value of knowledge (philosophy), studies of life and culture (sociology) and studies of learners and learning theory (psychology). Philosophical sources include ontology (what is real), epistemology (what is true) and axiology (what is good). Sociological sources provide the basis of content for curricular and thus the school curriculum reflects the nature of the society. Culturally induced bias is a major concern of curriculum developers. Contributions to the curriculum from the psychological point of view include formulation of educational objectives, understanding of the students' characteristics, the learning processes, teaching methods and evaluation procedures. Specifically, various institutions and scholars identify the content of curriculum as originating from various sources. Passigui (1999) notes the influences of essentialism and progressive schools in curriculum development processes. He argues that choice of content is influenced by the mind-set of a curriculum developer, for example essentialism, progressivism, etc.

Specific curriculum content source depends on curriculum developer and the way he or she views reality and curriculum. Essentialism is grounded in a conservative philosophy holding that schools should not try to radically reshape society. Rather, schools should transmit traditional moral values and intellectual knowledge that students would need to become model citizens. Essentialist curriculum developers therefore, would focus on traditional virtues such as respect for authority, fidelity to duty, consideration for others and practicality. They would place importance on science and understanding of the world through scientific experimentation. To convey important knowledge about the world, essentialist educators emphasize instruction in natural science rather than non-scientific disciplines such as philosophy or comparative religion. Curriculum developers in the essentialist school of thought focus their attention on the subject matter prepared by the teachers for the students to learn. Curriculum constitutes of permanent studies emphasizing for example the rules of grammar, reading, rhetoric, logic and mathematics for basic education. Measurements of outcomes are standard tests based on mastery of subject matter.

Progressivism, on the other hand, is a philosophical belief arguing that education must be based on the fact that humans are by nature social and learn best with others in real-life activities. Learning in isolation separates the mind from action. Certain abilities and skills can only be learned in groups, and social and intellectual interaction dissolves the artificial barriers of race and class by encouraging communication between various social groups. A progressive curriculum developer therefore focuses on students who should constantly learn by experimenting and solving problems; reconstructing their experiences and creating new knowledge. As such, teachers should not only emphasize drill and practice, but also expose learners to activities that relate to the real life situations of students. Curriculum is viewed as something flexible based on areas of interest. It is learner-centered and individual achievement is the factor of motivation. Generally, curriculum content is organized as lists of subjects, syllabi, courses of study or specific contents for the learner to actualize. Content is the total learning experience of the learner and as such measurement of outcomes are devices taking into considerations the subject matter and personality values.

CHAPTER - 4
DEVELOPMENT OF CURRICULUM

Curriculum Development Curriculum development means a continuous or never ending process. Its outcome is known through student's achievement of learning. Its assessment is made on the basis of change of behaviour of the learners. The learning experiences provide desirable change of behaviour of the pupils. They are evaluated with the help of examination. In curriculum development, the main focus of the curriculum is to develop the students. The curriculum is designed to realize the objective in terms of change of their behaviour. It is cyclic process 1. Teaching objectives, 2. Methods of teaching, 3. Examination and 4. Feedback.

1. Teaching Objectives: In view of subject objectives are identified as cognitive, affective and psychomotor. These objectives are written in behavioural terms. All learning experiences are organized to achieve these objectives.

2. Methods of Teaching: Teaching strategies are the most important aspect of providing learning experiences. The content is the means to select the method of teaching and level of the pupils.

3. Process of Evaluation: The evaluation of change of behaviour is made to ascertain about the realization of the teaching learning objectives. The level of pupil's performance indicates the effectiveness of method of teaching and learning experiences.

4. Feedback—the interpretation of performance provides the teacher to improve and modify the form of the curriculum. The curriculum is developed and teaching objectives are also revised The methodology of teaching is changed in view of the objectives to be achieved

Components of Curriculum Development
There are three components of educational process i e teacher, students and curriculum It has three type of objectives, cognitive, affective and psychomotor.. Educational process involves three major activities teaching, training and instruction.

According to B S Bloom, it is a triangular process (I) Educational process, (2) Learning experiences and (3) Change of behaviour. It is also a cyclic process; the teaching process is done through interaction between teacher and students. The curriculum is the basis for the interaction between teachers and taught.

Objective of Curriculum Development

1. Curriculum should provide the means for the all-round development of a child. Teaching should be organized with the help of curriculum.

2. Curriculum must involve the human experiences, culture and civilization which are to be transferred to new generation.

3. Curriculum should be the means to develop the moral character, discipline, honesty, cooperation, friendship, tolerance and sympathy with others.

4. Curriculum should help in developing the ability of thinking, wisdom, reasoning, judgment and other mental abilities.

5. It should consider the stages of growth and development of child for development attitude, interest, values and creative ability.

6. It should provide the awareness and understanding of physical and social environment and its components.

7. It should develop the right type of feeling and beliefs towards religions, new values and traditions.

8. It should help to develop democratic feeling and democratic way of life among students.

9. It should integrate the knowledge of various teaching subjects in view of their future life.

10. It should determine the mode of interaction

between teacher and students in school. The mode of teaching is decided by the nature of curriculum.

Basic Elements of Curriculum Development
The educational process includes teaching, training and instructional activities. Teaching activities are performed by a Teacher. They are planned or designed by the teacher according to four components (1) Teaching-learning objectives (2) Teaching content or subject matter (3) Teaching method and (4) Evaluation of learning outcomes. In the curriculum development, the level of students, the needs of the society and nation, the nature of content and means of providing learning experiences are considered as important factors. These are essential in identifying the objectives of teaching-learning. Several types of teaching objectives are attained by the same content. Each content has its own structure. Teaching is organized from memory to effective level on the same content of subject matter. The specific or behavioural objectives are realized by organizing specific teaching tasks and activities. Thus, curriculum development involves four basic elements (1) Objectives (2) Content (3) Method or strategies of teaching, and (4) Evaluation. These elements are interdependent.

1. Objectives: The subject's content structure, levels of students and type of examination components are considered in the identification of objectives of teaching and learning. These objectives are specific. These are written in behavioural terms so as to develop learning structures and conditions.

2. Content of Subject matter: The content of any subject is usually broad. It is analyzed into sub-content and into elements. These elements are arranged in a logical sequence. The behavioural objectives are written with the help of these elements of the content It is also known as logic of teaching.

3. Strategy of teaching: Specific objectives of teaching are attained with the help of appropriate teaching strategy. The behavioural objectives provide the awareness and insight about the specific learning conditions. The strategy is employed for providing learning experiences and bringing desirable behavioural change.

4. Evaluation: The level of student's attainment is evaluated by employing criteria referenced test. It shows the effectiveness of strategy of teaching and other components. The interpretation of evaluation provides the feedback to the curriculum and its components.

These are improved and modified to attain the objectives of teaching and learning. It is the empirical basis for the curriculum development. NCTE planned and prepared transaction of curriculum in 1995. After two years, it was realized that it needs modification and improvement. NCTE revised the B.Ed. courses in 1997. This is known as curriculum development. The difference between curriculum transaction and curriculum development has been summarized in the following table.

Transaction V/s Development of Curriculum

It is a broad concept and area of curriculum.	It is a specific and narrow concept of curriculum.
Management of curriculum is done at initial stage of introduction of new courses at school stages and higher levels.	Curriculum development is a cyclic process used for improving and modifying the courses at particular state of level.
3. Management of curriculum employs the following steps. (i) Planning,	It is a cyclic process using the following four steps. (i) Objectives,

(ii) Organizing, (iii) Administering, (iv) Guiding and, (v) Controlling.	(ii) Instructional methods, (iii) Evaluation and, (iv) Feedback.
Transaction of curriculum is a much more difficult task because it involves planning and preparing the course of discipline at school and university level.	It is used for specific course for specific stage. Relatively it is an easy and simple task.
Curriculum management is one by boards of study and boards of education. In some discipline councils plan and control. At university level there are Boards of studies for , different subjects.	Curriculum development is done by board of studies. The new courses and content are also included in revised curriculum. On the basis of try out the new courses.
It is based on theoretical aspect.	It is a continuous process based on practical aspect of curriculum.

CHAPTER - 5
MODELS OF CURRICULUM
DEVELOPMENT

INTRODUCTION
The excellence in the program in any institution reflects the quality of program planning and development. Education is no exception: the quality of individual school programs varies quite directly with the quality of program planning. The programs of individual schools, classrooms and of individual students usually mirror distinctly the nature and extent of the planning and development of these programs by teacher and students (Saylor and Alexander, 1966).

Curriculum development is a complex undertaking. Its complexity and difficulty are perhaps heightened by the usual absence of a set of clear ideas or models and planning and the how and theory of curriculum planning and development (Beauchamp, 1961).

ASSUMPTIONS OF CURRICULUM PLANNING (Saylor and Alexander, 1966)
1. Quality in educational program has priority in educational goals.

2. The curriculum itself must be dynamic and ever changing as new developments and needs in our society arise.
3. The process of curriculum planning must be continuous, not limited and must be dynamic.
4. No master curriculum plans will serve all schools.
5. Many individuals participate in curriculum planning.
6. Procedures of curriculum planning vary from system to system, from school to school, and from classroom to classroom, but they must be logical, consistent and identifiable in each situation.

MODELS OF CURRICULUM DEVELOPMENT

The term "model" as discussed by Oliva (1982) rates with scenario as one of the most abused words in current English usage. While a scenario may turn out to be any plan or series of events, a model may be a tried or untried scheme. It may be a programmed solution to specific problems or it may be a microscopic pattern proposed for replication or a grander scale.

Some of the models are simple, others are very complex. Within a given area of specialization (administration, instruction, supervision, or curriculum development), models may differ but bear great similarities. The individual models are often refinements or revisions, frequently major, often minor, of already existing models.

The educational consumer, i.e., the practitioners to whom the model is directed has the heavy responsibility of selecting one model in their particular field. If the practitioners are not disposed to apply models they discovered, they may as well design their own or, as the case may be, to put all together and come out with a working model as guide in curriculum planning.

By examining models for curriculum development, we can analyze the phases the originators or authors conceived as essential to the process of curriculum development. A model must show phases or components, not people. The specification of curriculum goals must chart a progression of steps from departmental committee to school faculty curriculum committee or extended school committee, to principal, to district curriculum committee, to superintendent and to school board (Oliva, 1982).

THE TYLER MODEL

One of the best known models for curriculum development with special attention to the planning phases is shown in Figures 1 and 2.

Figure 1. Tyler's Model

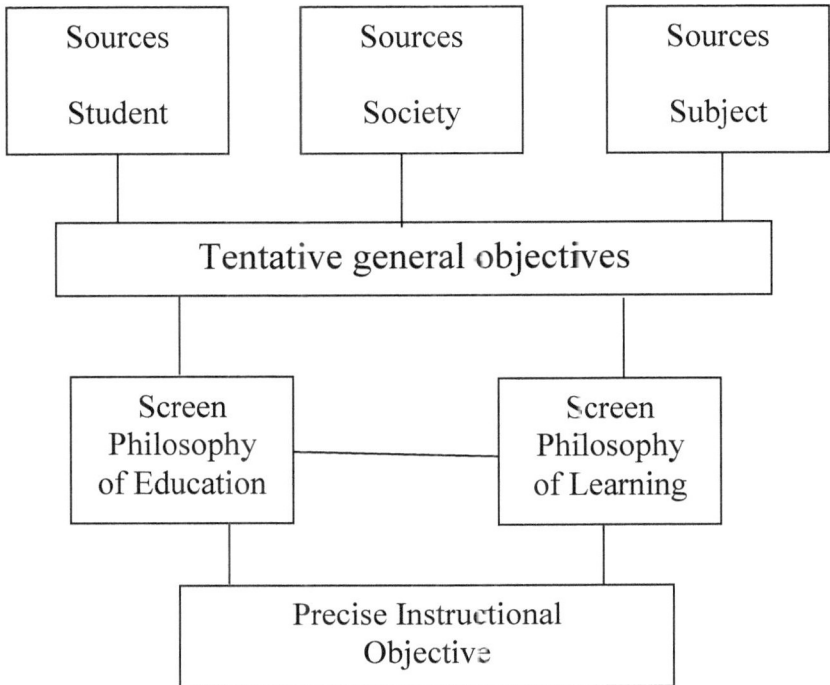

Sources Student	Sources Society	Sources Subject

Tentative general objectives

Screen Philosophy of Education	Screen Philosophy of Learning

Precise Instructional Objective

Figure 2. Tyler's model (expanded from Figure 1)

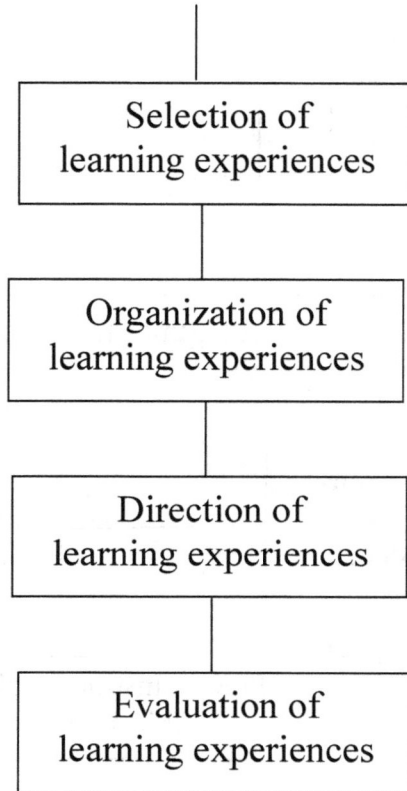

```
              |
  ┌───────────────────────┐
  │     Selection of      │
  │  learning experiences │
  └───────────────────────┘
              |
  ┌───────────────────────┐
  │    Organization of    │
  │  learning experiences │
  └───────────────────────┘
              |
  ┌───────────────────────┐
  │     Direction of      │
  │  learning experiences │
  └───────────────────────┘
              |
  ┌───────────────────────┐
  │     Evaluation of     │
  │  learning experiences │
  └───────────────────────┘
```

It proposed a comprehensive model for curriculum development. The first part of this model: the selection of objectives receives the greatest attention from other educators. Tyler recommended that curriculum planners identify general objectives by gathering data from the sources: the learners, contemporary life outside the school, and the subject matter. The numerous general objectives are refined by filtering them through two screens: (1) educational and social philosophy of the school and (2) the psychology of learning and become specific instructional objectives.

In describing general objectives Tyler referred them as "goals", "educational objectives", and "educational purposes". He further stated that the curriculum worker must begin analyzing data relevant to student needs and interest. These are educational, social, occupational, physical, psychological and recreational. He recommended observations by teachers, interviews with students, interviews with parents, questionnaires and tests as techniques for collecting data about students. By examining these needs, the curriculum developer identifies a set of potential objectives.

The next step in the process of general objectives is the analysis of contemporary life in both the local community and the society. From the needs of society flow many potential educational objectives.

For the source the curriculum planner turns to the subject matter, the disciplines themselves. From the three aforementioned sources, curriculum planners derived a multiplicity of general or broad objectives. Once this array of possible objectives is determined, a screening process is necessary to eliminate unnecessary and unimportant and contradictory objectives. Tyler advises the use of the schools educational and social philosophy as the first screen of these goals.

In Philosophical screen Tyler advise teachers of a particular schools to formulate educational and social philosophy and to outline values by emphasizing four democratic goals:

- the recognition of every individual as a human being regardless of his race, national, social and economic status;

- opportunity for wide participation in all phases of activities in the social groups in the society;

- encouragement of variability rather than demanding a single type of personality;

- faith and intelligence as a method of dealing with important problems rather than depending upon the authority of an autocratic or aristocratic group.

In the Psychological screen, the teachers must clarify the principles of learning that they believed to be sound. "A psychology of learning as emphasized by Tyler not only includes specific and definite findings but it unified formulation of theory of learning which helps to outline the nature of the learning process, how it takes place, under what conditions, what sort of mechanism operate and the like." Tyler explains the significance of the psychological screen in the following statements:

- Knowledge in the psychology of learning enables us to distinguish changes in human beings that can be expected to result from a learning process from those that can not.

- A knowledge in the psychology of learning enables us to distinguish goals that are feasible from those that are likely to take a very long time or are almost impossible of attainment at the age level contemplated.

- Psychology of learning gives us some idea of the length of time required to attain an objective and the age levels at which the effort is most efficiently employed.

In Fig. 2 Tyler's model describes three more steps in curriculum planning: selection, organization, and evaluation of learning experiences. He defined learning experiences as "the interaction between the learner and the external conditions in the environment to which he can react". And teachers must give attention to learning experiences in order to:

a) develop skill in thinking
b) helpful in acquiring information
c) helpful in developing social attitude
d) helpful in developing interest

THE LEYTON SOTO MODEL

Leyton Soto observed the linear nature of the Tyler model and the separation of the three sources of objectives. He eliminated some of the objectives to the Tyler model and added some of his refinements and clarifications as seen in Fig. 3. He charted three basic elements: philosophy, psychology and sources; three basic processes: selection, organization, and evaluation; and three fundamental concepts: objectives, activities, and experiences. Significantly he showed clearly the interrelationship among the various components of the model. He distinguished between learning experiences and learning activities. He defined objectives as the combination of experiences that the learner tries to achieve. Furthermore these experiences are the behaviors that are written into the objectives and activities are selected and organized, but only experiences, i.e. the terminal behaviors, are evaluated. Thus, the Leyton model presented an integrated or comprehensive model for curriculum development from the point of selecting objectives to the point of evaluating experiences.

THE TABA MODEL

Taba took what it is known as grassroots approach to curriculum development. She believed that the curriculum must be designed by teachers rather than handed down by higher authority. She felt that teachers should begin the process by creating specific teaching-learning units for their students rather than creating a curriculum design. She advocated an

Figure 3. Leyton Soto's integrated model

I. Basic elements

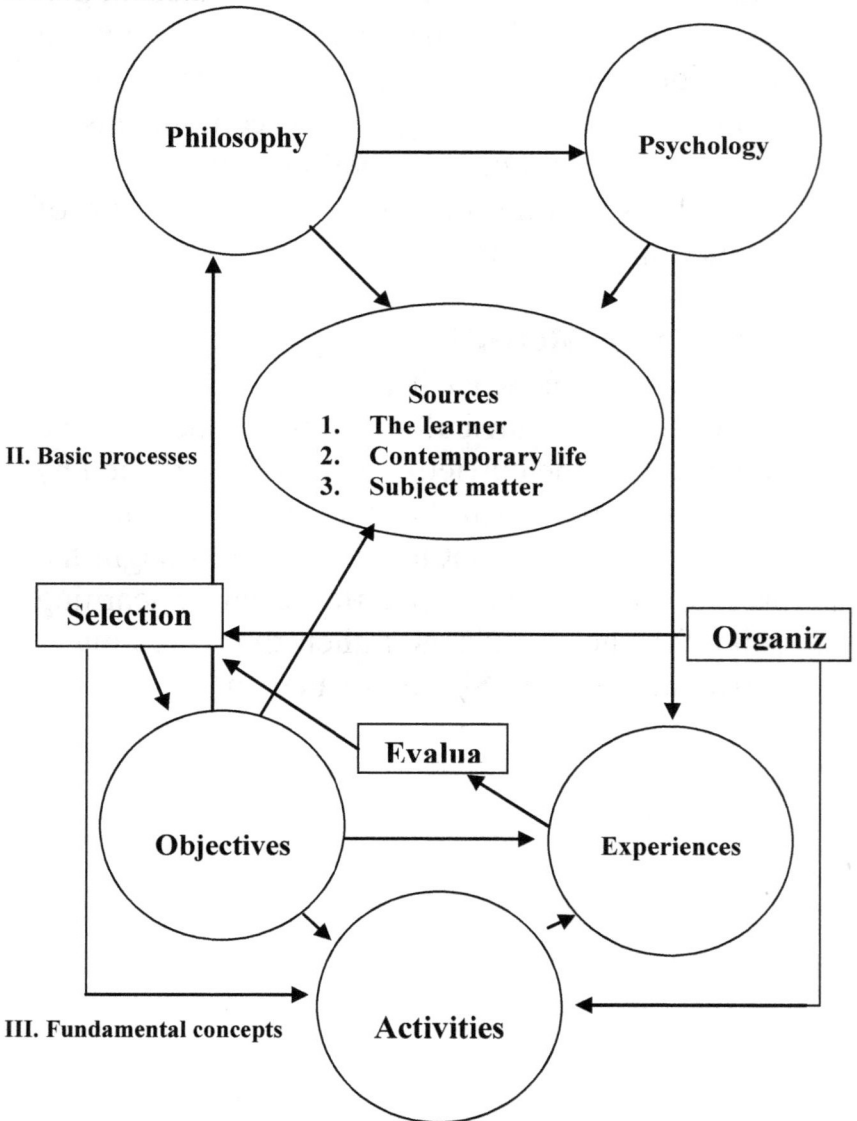

II. Basic processes

III. Fundamental concepts

Philosophy

Psychology

Sources
1. The learner
2. Contemporary life
3. Subject matter

Selection

Organiz

Evalua

Objectives

Experiences

Activities

inductive approach to curriculum development, starting with specifics and building up to general design and working down to specifics.

Taba's five steps sequence for accomplishing curriculum change.

1. Production by teachers of pilot teaching-learning units representative of the grade level or subject area.
   a. Diagnosis of needs.
   b. Formulation of objectives.
   c. Selection of content.
   d. Organization of content.
   e. Selection of learning experiences.
   f. Organization of learning experiences.
   g. Determination of what to evaluate and the ways and means of doing it.
   h. Checking for balance and sequence.
2. Testing experimental units.
3. Revising and consolidating.
4. Developing a framework.
5. Installing and disseminating new units.

THE SAYLOR AND ALEXANDER MODEL

Figure 4 shows the curriculum process in the model of Saylor and Alexander. Their definition of curriculum is "a plan for providing sets of learning opportunities to achieve broad educational goals and related specific objectives for an identifiable population served by a single school center. "Yet it is not to be conceived as a single document but rather as many smaller plans for particular portions of the curriculum".

Figure 4. Saylor and Alexander model

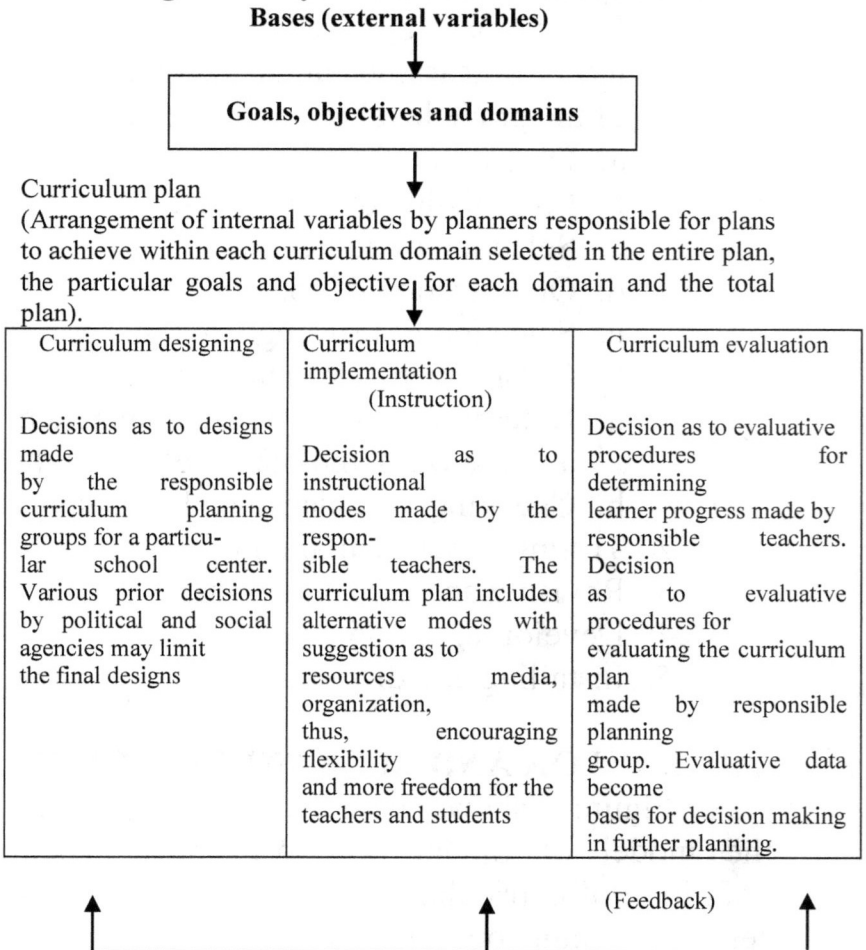

Bases (external variables)

↓

	Goals, objectives and domains	

Curriculum plan ↓
(Arrangement of internal variables by planners responsible for plans to achieve within each curriculum domain selected in the entire plan, the particular goals and objective, for each domain and the total plan). ↓

Curriculum designing	Curriculum implementation (Instruction)	Curriculum evaluation
Decisions as to designs made by the responsible curriculum planning groups for a particular school center. Various prior decisions by political and social agencies may limit the final designs	Decision as to instructional modes made by the respon-sible teachers. The curriculum plan includes alternative modes with suggestion as to resources media, organization, thus, encouraging flexibility and more freedom for the teachers and students	Decision as to evaluative procedures for determining learner progress made by responsible teachers. Decision as to evaluative procedures for evaluating the curriculum plan made by responsible planning group. Evaluative data become bases for decision making in further planning.

↑   ↑   (Feedback)   ↑

42

Goals, Objectives and Domain

The model indicates that the curriculum planners begin by specifying the major educational goals and specific objectives they wished to accomplish. Each major goal represents a curriculum domain.

The goals and objectives are selected after consideration of external variables, among which are legal requirements, educational research, regional accreditation standards, views of community groups and others.

Instructional Modes

At this point of the model, the teachers would then specify the instructional objectives before selecting the strategies or modes of the presentation.

Evaluation

Finally, the curriculum planners and teachers engage in evaluation must choose from a wide variety of evaluation techniques. Alexander and Saylor urge a comprehensive approach to evaluation that would permit assessment of the total educational program of the school and must include the curriculum plan, The effectiveness of instruction, and the achievement of the learners. Through evaluation processes, curriculum planner can determine whether or not, the goals of the school and the objectives of the school have been met.

THE OLIVA MODEL

The model shown in Figure 5 represents the most essential components that can be readily expanded into extended model that provides additional detail and simplified process.

Another Oliva's model is shown in Figure 6. It is a comprehensive; step by step process that takes the curriculum planner from the sources of curriculum to evaluation. It has

Figure 5. A model for curriculum development (Oliva, 1976)

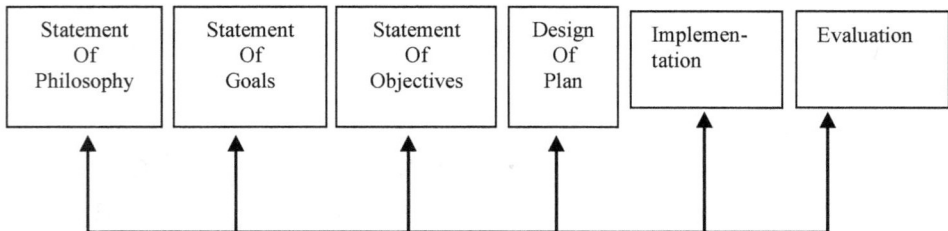

Statement Of Philosophy	Statement Of Goals	Statement Of Objectives	Design Of Plan	Implemen- tation	Evaluation

twelve components. The square represents planning phases and the circles, operational phases.

In Component I, it states the aim of education and their philosophical and psychological principles. These aims are beliefs that are derived from the needs of the individual

44

and society, which incorporate concept similar to Tyler's "screen".

Components II requires an analysis of the needs of the community in which the schools are located as well as the needs of the students and the exigencies of the subject matter that will be taught in school.

Components III & IV call for specifying curricular objectives based on Components I & II. The tasks of Component V are to organize and implement the curriculum, to formulate and establish the structure by which the curriculum will be organized.

In Components VI & VII an increasing level of specification is sought. Instructional goals and objectives are stated for each level of the subject. At this point it distinguish how the goals and objectives differ.

Component VIII shows how the curriculum worker chooses instructional strategies for use with students in the classroom. Simultaneously, the curriculum worker initiates Phase A of Component IX, Preliminary selection of evaluation technique. At this stage, the planner thinks ahead and begins to consider ways she will asses students' achievement. The implementation of instructional strategies follows-Component X.

Component XI is the stage when evaluation of instruction is carried out. Component XII completes the cycle with evaluation not of the student or of the teacher but rather of the curricular program.

The important features of the model are the feedback lines that cycle back from the evaluation of the curriculum to the curriculum goals and from the evaluation of instruction to the instructional goals. These lines indicate the necessity of continuos revision of the components of the respective subcycles.

SUMMARY

Five models of curriculum development are presented in this report. Models which can help us educators, planners and administrators to conceptualize a process by certain principles and procedures. Some models are embellished with diagram, others are simply lists of steps that are recommended to curriculum workers.

Those who take leadership in curriculum development are encouraged to become familiar with various models, to try them out, and to select and develop a model that is most understandable and feasible to them and to the persons with whom they are working.

In looking of various models we cannot say that any model is inherently superior to all other models. Some planners have followed one model, which they used for considerable length of time with considerable success. On the other hand, it does not mean that model represents the ultimate in models for curriculum improvement or that all educators are satisfied with it.

According to Oliva, (1986) he pointed that before choosing a model or designing a curriculum, curriculum planners should attempt to outline the criteria they would look for in a model for curriculum improvement. A model must show the following component: 1) major components of the process; 2) Customary, but not inflexible, "beginning and ending" points; 3) the relationship between curriculum and instruction; 4) distinction between curricular and instructional goals; 5) reciprocal relationship between components; 6) a cyclical rather than a linear pattern; 7) feedback lines; 8) the possibility of entry at any point of the cycle; 9) an internal consistency and logic; 10) enough simplicity to be intelligible; 11) components in the form of a diagram or chart.

Furthermore, the function of a curricular model must accomplish two purposes: 1) suggests a system to follow; 2) serve as the framework for explanation of phases or components of the process for curriculum improvement.

IMPLICATION

Curriculum development models are very important in guiding teachers, administrators and educational planners to verify whether the institution is implementing the needs of the clientele they are serving.

Every model has its own goals and objectives based from the needs of individuals, community and the society as a whole. The implementation process lies on the teachers as disseminators of learning and education.

No matter how simple or complicated model is the process of implementation lies the life of any curricular model. One must take into consideration that whatever model wants to adapt use, some maybe good for one, but some do not follow suit.

In this case, educators must not confine only to just one model but be receptive to other types of models, that one thinks will suit to the type of curriculum offerings.

Home Economics is a curriculum, which contribute to the improvement of human beings and society. Its aim and goals are oriented in this direction; improvement of life. In this regard, the Home Economics curriculum must always evaluate its goals and objectives. Realign if necessary these goals and objectives to the needs of the students, community and society to fit in with the new technology that are taking place in the world. The curriculum must be dynamic and adaptable to change, versatile and practical to be readily implemented.

At this point, teachers as implementors of change must be ready to accept changes, willing to learn and adapt changes, must be knowledgeable to current issues and the needs of the students, community and society as a whole.

The incorporation of all these are necessary components of a good curriculum. Moreover, Home Economists must work hand and hand, cooperate with each other for the improvement of the Home Economics curriculum.

As one Educator says "Education is one institution that plays a peculiar role in the preservation or the transformation of society". This role all the more very crucial considering mass education today. Given therefore, this role in education, Home Economists must take on the general task in promoting social transformation, value education and economic upliftment of the people.

The present task calls for teachers to be encouraged to participate seriously in the development of curriculum that would contribute to the ultimate improvement of the people it serve. And this is achieve only through organize efforts of each of us in the educational profession.

Another models which is well useful to teacher community is as under.

Administrative Model of Curriculum Development.

Meaning and Definition of Administrative Model of Curriculum Development Management refers to conscious preference from variety of alternative plus proposals and further the more that such choices involve purpose full commitment to recognize and derive objectives. Management employs strategies to achieve the objectives.

It indicates the various activities performed under the development of curriculum.

1. Planning a Curriculum.
2. Formulating Educational Objectives.
3. Organizing the Tasks.
4. Employing Strategies and Techniques.
5. Selecting and Appointing Workers.
6. Executing and coordinating among workers.

7. Evalualing and Controlling the Tasks.
8.Encouraging and Providing Feedback
Administrative model is related to management technology. Its broad outline is developed under 'Instruction design. The basis of 'managements involve the following five activities   1.Planning,   2.Organization, 3.Administration or Execution, 4. Guiding 5. Controlling of Feedback.

Education is a system which has various sub-systems. It is assumed that no system is perfect. Every system or subsystem needs improvement or development. The term 'curriculum development' refers to the improvement in the curriculum. I.K. Devies has designed and introduced "Managing Teaching Learning Approach' which involves four steps in educational process.
1.Planning of Teaching,
2. Organizing Teaching,
3. Leading of Teaching, and
4. Controlling Teaching.

The last step known as 'controlling teaching', means evaluation of objectives which provide the feedback for improving these steps. The planning includes managing curriculum and implementing curriculum. The basic model of curriculum depends on the objectives of

education.

Bases of Development of Curriculum

The development of curriculum is the commitment for realizing desired objectives of education. The objectives are based on various considerations and factors. The same considerations are equally important in planning or deciding the basic structure of curriculum. The following are the bases of transaction of curriculum.

1. Social philosophy of the society.
2. National needs or State needs.
3. Nature of course of study.
4. Type of examination system.
5. Form of the government.
6. Theory and assumptions of human organization.
7. Growth and development stage of students.
8. Recommendations of national commissions and committee of education.

The above basis of curriculum management and educational objectives are theoretical and practical. The last basis is more practical in transaction of curriculum. After independence, several commissions and committees have been established in Education- University education commission 1949. Secondary education commission (1952), National commission of education (1964-66) and

National Policy of education (1986) etc. These commissions have given the recommendations for managing curriculum or course of study for different stages.

Roles of Board of Education in Transaction of Curriculum

Management or Transaction of curriculum is a broad concept which includes the courses of study at school and +2 levels for different subject for different stage in pie-primary, primary, secondary and higher secondary. It is the function of CBSE Board, ICSE Board, and State Boards of education. India Education is on the state list. Every state of our country has its own system of education and state board of education. It is the responsibility of state board of education (SBE) to plan and prepare curriculum or courses of study. The state universities and central universities have academic autonomy plan and prepare courses of study for degree and post-graduate level for various subjects. Board of education, such as CBSE (Central Board of School Education) and ICSE (Indian Council of School Education) plan and prepare the courses of study for school and +2 levels.

Degree and postgraduate level courses of study are planned and prepared by the Boards of studies of universities. Technical and vocational courses are managed by the councils. National council of teacher-education has been functioning since 1995 and managing courses and programmes for teacher-education i.e., B.Ed. and M.Ed. courses of study. Some of such councils are:

1. N.C.T.E. - National Council of Teacher-Education
2. The Council of Medical Sciences i.e., for MBBS, M.D. and MS. at National level.
3. ICSSR and IARI Social Science and Agriculture Science.
4. The Law Council for L.L.B. and L.L.M.
5. The Council of Engineering Science B.E., M.E., B. Tech. and M. Tech.
6. National council of educational Research and training (NCERT).

System Analysis model of Construction and Development of Curriculum.
SYSTEM ANALYSIS:

System Analysis is closely related to both training psychology and cybernetic. It has emerged during Second World War. It has greatly influenced management decision making in business, industry, government and military. Known by serval terms, System Analysis had gained considerable standardization. Meaning of

System Analysis .The word system has been derived from the field of engineering. A system is the sum total of agents working independently and dependently together to achieve the required goals. The term 'system' conveys the meaning of analysis and development. The term 'system analyses emerged from the scientific management concept. In general it involves utilization of scientific mathematical techniques applied to organizational operation as a part of management decision making activities. It assumes that no comprehensive system development can take place without prior system analysis. It enables the administrators to use more scientific and quantitative methods for analyzing management problems. System technology brings to educational management a scientific-quantitative approach for solving complex educational administrative problems. **Procedure of System Analysis: The** following steps must be utilized for conducting system analysis study:

1. **First Step: Formulation of objectives:** To formulate the specific objectives to be achieved it is totally inadequate. To state objectives in general terms objectives may be written in behavioural terms or fiscal functions.

2. **Second Step: Review of system operation**: It

includes a comprehensive review of the system operation. System analysis is problem oriented. It is necessary to understand the system operation. The administrators do not always understand the main problem. Comprehensive review of the whole system is necessary to isolate the main problem to the solved.

3. Third Step: Collection of data: It involves the statistical techniques and procedure. In many situations, the aspects of system analysis are the application of classical statistical procedure.

4. Fourth Step: Analysis of data: It is done to make it meaningful. It is employed to experimental paradigms to study the effect of independent variable. An objective analysis is made for determining the influence of variables. The investigator is concerned with interaction of many variables. This primary concern is to be obtaining correlation not to establish cause and effect.

5. Fifth Step: Isolation of the problem: In order to isolate specific problem of the system, it is necessary to follow earlier steps. The collection and analysis of data helps in identil'ing and defining the problem.

6. Sixth Step: Specify operations in the problem: It is much more comprehensive than the original review of the total operations. It helps to under stand the relationship of all facts of the problem to the total operation system.

7. Seventh Step: Block Diagram: In the final step in the analytical stage of the systems analysis, a block diagram is prepared for all functions *of* the subsystem that make up problem area. It denotes logical structure of the sub-system operations and similar to the block diagram.

Design

After the system analysis, the investigator attempts to design and tentative solution of the problem. A new solution of the problem is subjected to testing. A tentative solution and retesting the tentative solution continues until an analyst reaches to an optimal solution. Once optimal solution is obtained, the analyst departs that loop.

Evaluation

The formal evaluation of the new solution is made for checking out its workability. It involves implementation of tentative solution in some aspect of the system. The analyst proceeds through the same steps of loop as mentioned earlier. It is advisable to evaluate all new system solutions in small scale of the required operations.

System Operations The new design has been implemented within the system for formal evaluation and acceptance for the solution of the problem. It involves two aspects:
1. Implementation of new system operation.
2. Maintenance of the system where a new system is designed.

Criteria for Evaluating
System Analysis Project

Performance, cost, utility and time are included in any **evaluation** system. The total system should operate in an optimal fashion. These criteria are of follows:

1. Performance: The effectiveness of a system evaluated on the basis of performance. The design of the problem solution ascertains how far the new system effective in achieving the objectives. The performance criterion is the concept of validity of the new system. The system is valid if it does what it is supposed to do. Thus, much of the evaluation of the performance is quantitative.

2. Cost: Analysis of system is influenced by cost function. The amount of resources is put into the system function in terms of money, staff and facilities.. Comparisons are made regarding the investment of resources in the new and old system of education. This is a valuable criterion

for evaluation system analysis projects.
3. Utility: The ultimate criterion for evaluating system project is utility of the system. The return on investment represents the utility of a given function. Many educational functions require an assignment of a numerical utility.

4. Time: Time factors as an evaluate criterion is closely associated with effectiveness. It is particularly relevant criterion in evaluating system projects. There is high correlation between time and cost. Much of the contribution of modem electronic data processing involves time.

Application of System Analysis in Education
The purpose of the system analysis is to get the "Best environment in the best place for the best people at the best time and in the best price"
"The system approach in instruction is an integrated, programmed complex of instructional media., hardware and personal whose components are structured as single unit with a schedule of time and sequential phasing."
The system analysis greatly influences the educational administration and organization. It provides scientific and quantitative basis for studying the problems of educational system. The educational implications of system analysis have been found in the following areas of

education.

1. Approach: It brings to educational management a scientific-quantitative approach for solving complex education administrative problems.

2. Problems: It enables educational administrator to identify the actual problem and abstains a verified solution of the problem.

3. Training: The training programmes can also be improved with the help of system analysis. The new concept of management may be implemented in training programmes.

4. Sub-systems: The Sub-systems of education is analyzed to understand the actual problem and tentative solutions can be verified or tested on a segment of the system.

5. Change: Any change in the educational system can be brought objectively, empirically and economically with great utility with the help of System Analysis.

System Approach System approach is a rational, problem- solving method of analyzing .the educational process and making it more effective. System is the process taken as a whole incorporating of all its aspects and parts, namely pupils, teachers, curriculum content, instructional materials, instructional strategies, physical environment and the evaluation of instructional objectives.

Keshaw and Michean (1959) have said "System approach is one of the techniques which aim at finding the most efficient and economically intelligent methods for solving the problems of education scientifically."

The system concept provides a framework for visualizing internal and external environmental factors as an integrated whole. It provides a way of thinking which helps us to recognize the nature of the complex problems and thereby, provides insight which enables us to operate within the received environment.

CHAPTER - 6
A REVIEW OF NATIONAL CURRICULUM FRAMEWORK FOR TEACHER EDUCATION

Every nation gives stress on teacher quality. Although teachers make a difference, there are many questions about how teachers are being prepared and how they ought to be prepared (USA NRC 2010, p.1). Effective curriculum frameworks for initial teacher training have their base in well defined standards for various categories of school teachers. A number of countries have developed standards for various levels of school teachers. Standards are essential to provide the basis for the formulation of the courses of studies. UK: TDA (2007) Professional Standards for Teachers in England, effective from September 2007, are available for five tasks: 1. Award of Qualified Teacher Status (QTS) (Q); 2. Teachers on the main scale (Core) (C); 3. Teachers on the upper pay scale (Post Threshold Teachers) (P); 4.Excellent Teachers (E); and 5. Advanced Skills Teachers (ASTs) (A). The standards are arranged in three inter-related sections: 1. Professional Attributes; 2. Professional Knowledge and Understanding; and 3. Professional Skills. In the USA, professional standards for teachers and school leaders vary from State to State. Its State of New Jersey has 10 different sets of standards and each standard has three components:

(a) Knowledge, (b) Disposition and (c) Performance.

In India, although national or state level standards for various categories of school teachers and teacher trainees are not available, at the national level, there have been three printed curriculum framework documents. The first printed curriculum framework for teacher education was brought out in 1978 (NCERT 1978). After ten years, in 1988 NCERT brought out a curriculum framework in cyclostyled form (NCERT:NCTE 1988a &b). The National Council for Teacher Education, the statutory body of the Government of India for teacher education, brought out a printed version of curriculum framework in 1998 (NCTE 1998). After bringing out a curriculum framework for school education in 2000, NCERT brought out a curriculum framework for teacher education in 2004 (NCERT 2004). After NCERT modified its School Curriculum Framework in 2005, NCTE and NCERT jointly brought out a Discussion document for Curriculum Framework in 2006(NCTE-NCERT 2006). Basing on the feedbacks received, NCTE attempted to bring out a new version of curriculum framework, which resulted in two incomplete documents - one in 2007 (NCTE 2007) and the other in 2008 (NCTE 2008). Finally, towards the end of 2009, NCTE published "National Curriculum Framework for Teacher Education: Towards Preparing Professional and Humane Teacher", which is being reviewed here.

In order to develop teacher training curricula, many nations carry out sample evaluation of their teacher training programmes. They study the opinions of the stake holders such as the directors of school education in the states, school inspectors, school managers and heads of schools. During 2000-2005, the American Educational Research Association commissioned a 14-member panel to study teacher education policies and practices, especially the impact on professional performance, students of learning and other important school outcomes (Cochran-smith & Zeichner 2005). The areas covered by the study were: (a) Teacher education in changing times: politics and paradigms; (b) Teacher characteristics: the demographic profile and the indicators of quality; (c) Effects of coursework in the arts and sciences and the foundations of education; (d) Methods courses and field experiences; (e) Pedagogical aspects ;

(f) Preparing teachers for diverse populations; (g) Preparing general education teachers to work with students with disabilities; (h) Accountability processes in teacher education; and (i) Teacher education programmes. The Report has also suggested a research agenda for teacher education. While reporting promising lines of research, the document stated that •g•c the body of teacher education research that directly addresses desirable pupil and other outcomes and the conditions and contexts within which these outcomes are likely to occur is relatively small and inconclusive• (p.5). A recent study conducted by the National Research Council of the USA commissioned by the US Department of Education suggested research on the sources of the variation in traditional and alternate mode of teacher preparation in respect of preparation, such as selectivity, timing, and specific components and characteristics. It did not appreciate current mechanisms for accountability and quality control in teacher education in USA and suggested an independent evaluation by the US Department of Education (US:NRC 2009, p.3). A study of teacher education in Canada (Crocker, Duibbon & Raham 2008) conducted during 2007-2008, covered(a) Structure, (b) Content, (c) Teaching

65

knowledge and skills, (d) The practicum, (e) Preparedness for teaching, and (e) Collaboration with the school. The data were obtained from surveys of representative samples of recent graduates, school principals and education faculty members. The study pointed out necessity for undertaking large scale, longitudinal and comparative studies and developing a common vision for teacher education which articulates core content and competencies, finding better ways to support and mentor novice teachers, and developing stronger models of collaboration between faculties of education and the school system they serve (p.11). In Indian situation, during late nineties, NCTE was able to bring out State reports on teacher education. These might have given inputs for development of curriculum framework of 1998. Such an exercise might have been useful for the teacher education curriculum, developed after a decade. Findings of studies comparing initial teacher training curricula of various States and UTs with the curricula in developed countries might have benefited the present curriculum framework document.

The Curriculum Framework of Teacher education of 2009 has six chapters. The first chapter •"Context, concerns and vision of teacher education" deals with (a) The changing school context and its demands;

Present teacher education scenario; (c) Teacher education reform perspectives: past and present; (d) Systemic concerns of teacher education; (e) Professionalisation of teacher education; (f) Preparing teacher educators; (g) Research and innovation; (h) Open and distance learning in teacher education; (i) Education of teachers in health and physical education; (j) Education of teachers for vocational education; and (k) Vision of teachers and teacher education. This chapter has mentioned about decline in the quality of the State school system. •"Increasing privatisation and differentiation of the school system have vitiated drastically the right to quality education for all children" (p.4). Privatisation is taking place with the approval of the government. Hence, it might have been better, if the document would have mentioned about the strategies to be followed by the examining bodies to ensure quality in initial teacher training, in view of large scale privatisation in certain States and UTs. The document has stated that •"para teachers pose a far more serious challenge to the provision of free and compulsory education of quality to all children" (pp.5-6). Para teacher scheme is a government scheme. Instead of criticising the scheme, it would have been better, if the document would have mentioned about the strategies to be followed by the government agencies to provide initial training to these para teachers. The document has also highlighted the curricular burden on school children and lack of coherence in the curriculum structure often dissociated from the personal and social milieu of children (p.4). It might have been better, if the document would have mentioned the strategies to be employed in initial teacher training programmes to develop the skills in the teacher trainees for tackling the curriculum load issues. School curricula are framed by various national and state level school boards. The document has pointed out merits of National Curriculum Framework developed by NCERT (p.4) and has discussed about deterioration of the quality of school education, but has not discussed strategies to develop skills in teacher trainees to check deterioration of the system. The document has mentioned about problems in teacher preparation such as failure to make connections with children and respond to their needs and imaginative ways (p.4). It has mentioned that •"dilution of emphasis on public investment in initial teacher education since the 1990s has led to a large scale recruitment of unqualified and under-qualified persons in the formal school system" (p.6). Such criticisms are based on observation of a few practices, but cannot be generalised, especially, when findings of national level evaluation of quality of initial teacher training programmes are not available. Commenting on function of centrally sponsored scheme of teacher education, the document has stated that •"The capacity of both CTEs and IASEs in performing their mandated roles has more recently come under serious scrutiny" (p. 5). This criticism on the central government scheme may be valid, but is irrelevant for this document on teacher training curriculum. At page 8, while discussing elementary teacher education reform, the document has stated that •"The Curriculum Frameworks thus far developed provide guidelines that are too general and do not address the stage specific training needs of elementary teachers. The Curriculum Framework for Quality Teacher Education (1998) was perhaps the first to have provided stage- specific guidelines". These statements might have been suitably refined, to make them clearer.

The second chapter "Curricular areas of initial teacher preparation" gives a flow chart of the proposed curricular areas. The curricular area: A -'Foundations of Education' covers (a) Childhood, child and adolescent development and learning; (b) Contemporary studies: (i) teacher and learner in society; and (ii) gender, school and society; (c) Educational studies: i) aims of education, knowledge and values; (ii) developing the self and aspirations as a teacher. The curricular area B •'Curriculum and Pedagogy' covers (a) Curriculum studies: (i) knowledge and curriculum; and (ii) language proficiency and communication; (b) Pedagogic studies: School knowledge, learner and pedagogy; and (c) Assessment and evaluation studies. The curricular area C covers School internship. The document then discusses on •"Time as a critical factor in teacher preparation". Next, it discusses certain •"commonly held" criticisms (p.45). These criticisms may be true for specific situations, but may not be applicable for all programmes and institutions. The document has stated that •"It is perhaps high time that we pay heed to the specific suggestion of increasing the duration of initial teacher education, recommended by the two most significant policy Commissions of post-independence India, namely the Kothari Commission (1964-66) and the Chattopadhyaya

70

Commission 1983-85"(p.45). The actual wordings found in the Report of the Education Commission 1964-66 are:

"At the secondary stage, where the duration of the course is only one year, it has been suggested that it should be increased to two years, to do justice to the existing heavy courses. From a financial and practical point of view, this does not seem feasible. However, it is possible to make better use of the existing duration by extending the working days in the academic year from the existing level of 180-190 days to 230 days." (Kothari 1966, Art.4.15, p.132)

The National Commission on Teacher Education I, after coming to conclusion that more time be made available for B.Ed. programme stated that •"We are of the view that the two summer months may be added to the academic year ensuring a working year of 220 days. An increase in the working hours per day may also be considered" (Chattopadhyaya 1985, Art. 7.09, p.49). As part of 'Redesigning current teacher education programmes', the framework document has suggested that •"initial teacher education be of 4 year duration after senior secondary; or 2 years duration after a Bachelor's degree programme•h (p. 46), without noticing that number of years, a teacher trainee, after passing sr. secondary, spends in the first case is four years and in the second case, it is five years. Hence, these two course products may not be accepted as equivalent. After explaining the teacher education curricular areas table, the document has given example of a four year integrated programme offered by the University of Delhi. It would have been better if the document would have quoted findings of studies which have indicated effectiveness of such a programme. It has stated that in case of DIETs, •"the faculty appointed does not possess qualifications or experience in elementary teacher education". It has failed to mention about necessity for school teaching experience of the faculty of secondary teacher education institutions although Kothari (1966, p. 129) and Mudaliar (1953, p.168) pointed out such necessities. Mudaliar (1953, p. 167) even suggested that M.Ed. courses should admit trained graduate teachers having normally a minimum of three years teaching in a school. The NCTE document, being reviewed, in its suggested Redesign for D. Ed. two year Diploma after +2 and one year B. Ed. degree after graduation, has mentioned three areas: A: Foundations of education, B: Curriculum and pedagogy and C: School internship. The school internship has suggested •"Visits to innovative centres of pedagogy and learning, wherever feasible" (p.48). This statement indicates that the Framework has not made this visit compulsory for all. The document has mentioned school internship for 4 days a week. It has not explained what is wrong with the system where internship is provided on all the working days continuously. It also has not stated in what manner the remaining days of the week are to be utilised. It has suggested a minimum period of 6-10 weeks including an initial phase of observing a regular classroom. The document has suggested minimum duration of internship of 6-10 weeks for a two year programme and 15-20 weeks for a four year programme. It has not spelt out the reasons for which it has suggested a range in duration. It might have been better, if the document would have spelt out the reasons for which, the document has suggested variation in ranges of school teaching experience between two year programme and four year programme; although the products are expected to do the same work. On the same page, the document has stated that "While functioning as a regular teacher for a sustained period of a minimum 12-20 weeks, the interns would get an opportunity to learn to ...(p.41). The duration mentioned here does not match with the duration suggested earlier, on the same page 41. The document has not clarified the difference. The document has suggested 4 unit plans per subject. The first printed curriculum framework for teacher education (NCERT 1978) had mentioned three areas in its proposed teacher education programmes - (a) Pedagogical theory (20%), (b) Working with community (20%) and (c) Content-cum-methodology and practice teaching including related practical work (60%). The weightages for pre-school, primary and secondary teacher education programmes were same. In case of higher secondary and collegiate courses, the weightages were a (30%), b (20%), and c (50%). Subsequent curriculum frameworks including the present one have not mentioned the weightages and have not given special status to 'Working with community'. The suggestion for separate courses for initial teacher training for teaching higher secondary and collegiate stages found in certain earlier curriculum frameworks has not been found, in case of the present NCTE document.

The third chapter is •"Transacting the curriculum and evaluating the developing teacher" gives a table comparing the dominant current practices and proposed process based teacher education

curriculum framework. Its section on transacting the teacher education curriculum discusses aspects: (a) Teaching the adult learner; (b) Bringing the learners•f own experience centre-stage; (c) Engagement with theoretical concepts and frameworks, (d) Training to be reflective practitioners; (e) Theory-practice dialectic, and (f) Meaningful internship and school experience. In its section on Need for complementary structures and mechanism, it has suggested establishment of Teacher Learning Centres (TLC) in every teacher training institution. As per the document has stated that a TLC would provide (a) Structural space for hands-on experience; (b) A resource for teacher trainees, teacher practitioners and teacher educators;
(c) A forum for innovation and sharing; (d) A platform for classroom-based research; (e) A structural space for self-directed activities; (f) A platform for developing a repertoire of skills; (g) A structural space for the personal and psychological development of teachers; and (h) A structural space for forging links between pre-service and in-service teacher education. The section on •'Evaluating the developing teacher' has made brief discussion on the comprehensive nature of evaluation. The section on •'evaluation protocol' has covered areas: (a) Observing

learners for a specified duration in specific situations; (b) Observational records maintained by the student teacher on a set of criteria relevant to the task and report writing; (c) School contact practicum to relate and communicate with the learner; (d) Planning for the school contact; (e) Post contact discussions, report writing and group presentations; (f) Psychological and professional development of the teacher; (g) Assessing a repertoire of skills; (h) Understanding the learner, curricular and pedagogic issues; (i) Teacher as researcher; (j) Internship activities on which students (student teachers?) may be assessed; and (k) Reflective journal. At the end of this chapter, the document has discussed on •'Designing instruments of evaluation and assessment' and •'Preparation of a scheme for continuous and comprehensive evaluation'.

The fourth chapter •"Continuing professional development and support for in-service teachers" would have been more appropriate as a separate document, may be with the title •"Guidelines for Continuing Professional Development and Support for Teachers". In the •'Introduction' section, the Curriculum framework document has stated that •"Following the Kothari Commission Report, school clusters were created in several states to forge inter-linkages between primary, middle and high schools' (p.63). But Kothari Commission had suggested •'School complexes'. not •'school clusters'. A few other statements that might not be accepted by all sections of the teacher education community are:

Teachers' involvement in textbook preparation and indeed even in the preparation of training modules has grown over the years. Teachers themselves have opportunities to work in the Block and Cluster Resource Centres as well as to contribute to training as Resource persons. They are also members of committees formulating educational policies. NGO initiatives in several parts of the country have developed and implemented models of teacher professional development and support in ways that directly impact the classroom practice.•h(p.64)

The document has criticised the effectiveness of government run in-service programmes. •"Evidence of •'effectiveness' of training programmes and support activities, especially within the government system, continues to be only anecdotal and impressionistic, and even contrary, depending on who is asking the questions or doing the observation"(p.64). The second section of this chapter has dealt with aims of continuing professional development programmes for teachers. Third section has covered •'Designing inservice programmes: some principles'. The fourth section •'Routes towards teachers' continuing professional development' has suggested short and long term courses. While recommending provision for sabbatical for study and research, it has suggested encouragement for small research projects and case studies through which teachers can reflect on, share and develop their practice. The document has stated that "At the same time, the insistence that teachers must carry out action research is not productive, particularly in a context where there is little understanding of action research, and virtually, no forum to share such research"(pp.68-69). This statement appears odd in view of the fact that on pages 27 and 37; the document has recommended classroom based research that includes action research. The document has suggested encouragement for participation in professional conferences and meetings, providing professional fora, resource rooms and materials; and making provision for faculty exchange visits and fellowships. Discussion on •'Organization of continuing professional development programmes' carried out in the fifth section deals with (a) Organisation and coordination; and (b) Sites and agencies. The section 6 covers

•'Impact' and the last section covers•'Structural and operational issues of continuing professional development'.

The fifth chapter "Preparing teacher educators" might have been more justified as a separate document. NCERT (1988, p. iii) stated that •"It excludes M. Ed. / M. Phil. / M. A. (education) programmes as these are not considered primarily as teacher preparation courses". The chapter 5 of the present NCTE document has eight sections. In the first section 'Introduction', the document has stated about shortage of properly qualified and professionally trained teacher educators. This assumption may not be true; as such candidates prefer to work in schools than join private teacher training institutions which pay salary less than the school teachers. In the second section, the document has discussed basic issues of education of teacher educators: (a) Teacher educators and school education; and (b) Stage specificity in the preparation of teacher educators. Here, the document has discussed how elementary education remains sadly neglected as knowledge field and refers to efforts of NGOs. Perhaps such a discussion does not fit into the theme of education of teacher educators. It has stated that "...the M.Ed. programme in most of the universities neither widens nor deepens the discourse of education at the secondary stage that students bring with them after their B.Ed. degree"(p.78). The document has not stated how it has come to such a conclusion. The third section is •"M.Ed. as a programme for preparation of teacher educators". It has pointed out problems in having M.A.(Education) as a teacher educator preparation programme by stating that •"The existence of two parallel post graduate programmes in education has created an anomalous and confusing situation and has raised questions of equivalence"(p.79). In support of its argument, it has quoted NCF position paper on teacher education. As there is wide variation among M.Ed. programmes, similarly, there can be variation between M. Ed. and M. A. (Education) programmes. There are many Professors of Education who have studied M. A. (Education) not M. Ed. Hence, there should not be any confusion in treating these two courses as equivalent. In the fourth section ,'Imparting professionalism to a post graduate programme in education', the document has suggested discourse to be initiated in certain aspects including •"broad basing the profile of teacher educators by infusion of persons who have the knowledge of disciplines generic to teacher education so that the discipline of education grows into specialization requiring persons to be well-versed in cognate disciplines outside education" (P. 80). Such a statement supports the States and UTs which has not made M. Ed. or M.A. (Education) degree compulsory for lecturers and principals in their colleges of education. This statement is perhaps a set back to the attempt to have separate cadre for teacher educators, who have either M.Ed. or M.A. (Education) degrees. The fifth section •"Needed thrusts for development of teacher educators" has covered (a) Early childhood education; (b) Primary / elementary education; and (c) Secondary education. On page 81, the document has stated that •"In most states, DIETs are the main supply institutions for elementary teachers". As non-DIET elementary teacher training institutions are more than five times of number of DIETs as per NCTE, such a statement may be wrong. The document refers to privatisation, although privatisation of elementary or secondary teacher education is not found in each State and UT. While discussing about faculty of the DIETs, the document points out that •"Many of them do not possess basic experience in primary school teaching" (p.82). The document has been silent about the status of school teaching experience of teacher educators working in the departments of education in the university and general colleges and in the colleges of education and the Departments of Education of Regional Institutes of Education of NCERT. Pointing out importance of school teaching experience, the University Education Commission 1948-49 had stated that "If it is argued that, as things are, it is difficult to find school teachers intellectually capable of holding lecturers' posts, the answer must be that nothing would so quickly rectify this state of affairs as the knowledge that you could not hope to be a lecturer or professor in education unless you had started by teaching in a school" (Radhakrishnan 1949, pp.143-144).

The Commission has also pointed out necessity of school teaching experience for M.Ed. students. It has stated that •"Normally, however, it would be better for a student to learn or more about the practice of education by teaching a few years before he returned to take the Master's Degree in the subject."(pp.143-144). The Secondary Education Commission 1952-53 also has stated that "We believe that it would be an advantage if for this higher degree in education trained teachers who have done normally a minimum of three years teaching in a school are only selected."(Mudaliar 1953, p. 167). NCERT (1978) has also suggested that •"the teacher-educators should themselves participate in classroom teaching cooperating schools to have first-hand experience of the actual conditions prevailing in schools"(p.10). The present curriculum framework document has been silent about this aspect of professional experience of teacher educators. The document has mentioned about M. Ed. (Elementary) course offered at Jamia Millia Islamia, New Delhi, but has not mentioned about findings of any study conducted on this programme and to what extent faculty members of JMI imparting this programme have direct experience or continued experience of elementary school teaching. In the sixth section "Encouraging innovations for preparation of teacher educators", the document has mentioned about M. A. Education (Elementary) launched by the Tata Institute of Social Sciences, Mumbai, but has not mentioned about findings of evaluation studies on this course. In the seventh section •'Enhancing the Status of educational studies and the professional development of teacher educators, the document has quoted ideas from the draft Curriculum Framework of 2006 and report of the working group for teacher education during the

XI plan. In the last section of this chapter, 'Preparation of teacher educators-future directions and possibilities', the document states that Reform of teacher education to move forward on a sound footing demands dedicated research in the area of foundations of education in the Indian context by universities, preferably in independently established departments. The research in such departments would help develop the teacher education programmes on a more sound theoretical basis. The existing departments of education have hardly been able to engage themselves in this long-pending need for their pre-occupation in conducting routine teacher training and research programmes" (p.87).

The above statements may not be valid. The last sentence of the above quotation has created confusion. The Association of Teacher Educators of USA has developed standards for teacher educators in 9 sections: 1. Teaching, 2. Cultural competence, 3. Scholarship, 4. Professional development, 5.Program development, 6. Collaboration, 7. Public advocacy, 8. Teacher education profession, and 9. Vision. Every section has indictors and artefacts. All these standards may not be applied to Indian system, as most of the teacher educators in USA are attached to concurrent model of teacher training, whereas in India, most of the teacher educators are attached to consecutive model of teacher training. Again, in India, schools do not play much role in supervising teacher trainees. This chapter has not mentioned standards for accomplished teacher educators which could have helped the teacher educator preparation programmes and also could have assisted employers of teacher educators. This document has not covered preparation of craft instructors, physical education instructors, art instructors, etc. posted as regular employees in many teacher training institutions.

In the last chapter "Implementation strategies", the present curriculum framework document has mentioned various measures to be taken by the NCTE. These include (a) Dissemination of the curriculum framework document; (b) Organisation of at least five consultation meetings in each region;(c) Facilitating revision of the existing teacher education programmes;(d) Discourse on the structural aspects of teacher education programmes; (e) Evolving adequate structural mechanisms to promote entry of talent in teacher education programmes; (f) Constitution of a working group of scholars to develop syllabi and course outlines, spelling cut objectives, distribution of courses, weightages etc.; (g) Catalytic role to be played by NCTE in development of textual materials, facilitating regional language versions; and (h) Encouragement to institutions to experiment with the innovative models. The document has stated that NCTE would initiate dialogue to have all teacher education programmes under the aegis of universities and would encourage four year programme of elementary teacher education. Such a dialogue for elevating primary school teacher training to degree level might have to consider possibility of doubling of expenditure in teacher salary and capability of the States and the central government to bear this financial burden, which might be not thought of as the government has not yet been able to expand pre-school education, in spite of the fact that it has been included in the Article 45 of the Directive Principles of the constitution. The dialogue might also explore possibility of having Diploma courses for primary school teacher training with the non lecturers as faculty members, operating in the university system, which shall not require extra expenditure on teacher salary. At the end, it has stated that "Existing B.Ed. programmes should be reviewed to facilitate the choice between a 4-year integrated model after +2 or a 2 year model after graduation, based on State requirements and available institutional capacity" (p.91) without taking into consideration the number of years one spends after +2. However, earlier it has stated that •"Teacher education programmes should ideally be of four-five years' duration after the completion of 10+2 level of school education" (p.90), indicating that it has not come to a decision about number of years. It has proposed separate exercises for preparation of teachers for the curricular area of health and physical education and also of vocational education. It has stated that NCTE would have a series of professional orientation / training programmes to expound the contours of learner studies, contemporary studies, educational studies and curriculum and pedagogic studies. NCTE would also initiate steps to ensure entry of talent in teacher education programmes. The document has suggested a study to assess dominant entry qualifications for pre-service programmes in elementary education, to design state specific strategies. It closes with the statement •"A nation-wide review of teacher education curriculum in the light of the selected curriculum renewal exercise would need to be undertaken" (p.92). This gives assurance for a bright future for efforts for qualitative improvement of teacher education by NCTE.

7. CONCLUSION

As each chapter of this document starts with an •'Introduction' section, it might have been better to close each chapter with a 'Conclusion' section. The document indicates that it has taken ideas from earlier documents and in doing that, it has created problems for itself. It has used varieties of terminologies for teacher trainees: 'student teachers'(p.59), 'pre-service students' (p.98), •'trainees' (p.61), 'intern' (p.61), •'students' (p.61) •'teacher' (p.60), and 'teacher trainees' (p.33). There have been also many repetitive criticisms. It seems the document has been printed hurriedly for which pages 22 and 88 have remained blank. It has quoted from many documents but has not mentioned the page numbers of the relevant publications. The •'End note and References' printed on the last page (p.93) has not covered a large number of documents cited in the text such as : Report of the University Education Commission 1948-49, Report of the Education Commission 1964-66, National Policy on Education 1986, National Curriculum Framework 2005, Right of Children to Free and Compulsory Education Act 2009, Curriculum Frameworks for Teacher Education of 1978, 1988, and 1998, Discussion Paper 2006, SSA

2002, DPEP 1995, OB 1986, National Commission on Teachers 1983-85 (I or II?), NPE Review Committee 1990, National Advisory Committee on Learning without Burden (1993), The Person with Disabilities Act 1996, and NCF 2005 Position Paper on Teacher Education. Too many references to the school curriculum framework of NCERT have created confusion. Of course, long quotations have contributed to increase the number of pages. It might have been better if the the document would have avoided use of •'we', •'our', etc. Curriculum Framework for Teacher Education of 1978 had 25 entries under Errata. The present curriculum document might have enriched itself by including •'Errata'. The •'Preface' to the document has stated the urgency •'to prune the theory and practice of teacher education' (p.iii). The document might have been pruned by avoiding support from government documents and individual writings. NCERT (1978) has mentioned objectives for each of the four stages: Pre-primary, Primary, Secondary and Higher secondary. NCTE (1998) has mentioned •'General objectives' and also mentioned •'Specific objectives' for teacher education for the stages of Early childhood, Primary, Elementary, Secondary, and Senior secondary.

This document might have improved itself by specifying objectives or expected standards for each category of initial teacher training. As the document conatins many factual errors as well as irrelevant statements, it may be better if a modified version of the document is brought out.

BIBLIOGRAPHY

Caswell H.L. Reading in curriculum development. NewYork: American Book Company.

Chattopadhyaya, D. P. (1985) (Chairman) *The Teacher and Society: Report of National Commission on Teachers I 1983-85.*Govt. of India, New Delhi.

Cochran-Smith, M. & Zeichner, K. M. (Editors) (2005) *Studying Teacher Education.* Lawerence Erlbaum, Mahwah.

Crocker, R., Dibbon, D. & Reham, H. (2008) *TeacherEducation in Canada.* Society for the Advancement in Education. Kelwona.

Good, Carter V. (1959)Dictionary of Education (Second Edition). New York : McGraw–Hill Book Co.

Harper & Row (1981) A Dictionary of education by Derek Rowntree.pp 354, London.

Hills, P.J. (Ed.).(1982).A dictionary of education. London: Routledge & Kegan Paul.

J. C. Aggarawall (1996:307-16)" Principles, Methods & Techniques of teaching

Kothari, D. S. (1966) (Chairman) *Report of the Education Commission 1964-66.* Govt. of India, New Delhi.

Mudaliar, A. L. (1953) (Chairman) *Report of the Secondary Education Commission 1952-53.* Govt. of India, New Delhi.

NCERT (1978) *Teacher Education Curriculum: A Framework Prepared for National Council for Teacher Education.* Author, New Delhi.

NCERT (2004) *Curriculum Framework for Teacher Education.* Author, New Delhi.

NCERT:NCTE (1988a) *Teacher Education Curriculum: A Framework.* NCERT, New Delhi.

NCERT:NCTE(1988b) *Teacher Education Curriculum: A Framework-Revised Draft.* NCERT, New Delhi.

NCTE (1998) *Curriculum Framework for Teacher Education.* Author, New Delhi.

NCTE (2007) *Curriculum Framework: Teacher Education for a Knowledge Society (Draft).* Author, New Delhi.

NCTE (2008) *Teacher Education Curriculum: Bases and Frameworks (Draft).* Author, New Delhi.

NCTE (2009a) *National Curriculum Framework for Teacher Education 2009 (Draft for Discussion).* Author, New Delhi.

NCTE (2009b) *National Curriculum Framework for Teacher Education: Towards Preparing Professional and Humane Teacher.* Author, New Delhi.

NCTE -NCERT (2006) *Curriculum Framework for Teacher Education(Draft).* NCTE, New Delhi.

National Research Council, Washington DC. Retrieved fromhttp://www.nap.edu/catalog/12882.html

Oliva P. F. (1982). Curriculum planning: Little, Brown

Peter Cochrane, Liz Diprose, Don Munro . (1996)Carlton, Inside out student guide Vic.: Curriculum Corporation.

Radhakrishnan, S. (1949) (Chairman) *Report of the University Education Commission 1948-49.* Govt. of India, New Delhi.

Ronald C. Doll (1970). Curriculum improvement: decision-making and process (2d ed.). Boston, Allyn and Bacon.

Saylor, John Galen; Alexander, William M.(1966).Curriculum Planning for Modern Schools. Carson City, NV, U.S.A:

UK TDA (2007) *Professional Standards for Teachers in England from September 2007.* Retrieved on 4 April 2010 from http://www.tda.gov.uk/upload/resources/pdf/s/standards_a4.pdf

US:NRC (2010) *Summary: Preparing Teachers: Building Evidence for Sound Policy (Study of Teacher Preparation Programs in the United States).*

www.ingramcontent.com/pod-product-compliance
Lightning Source LLC
Chambersburg PA
CBHW060402050426
42449CB00009B/1860